Teignmouth
in old picture postcards

by
Ann Pearson

European Library – Zaltbommel/Netherlands

Second edition: 1990

GB   ISBN 90 288 3367 6 / CIP

© 1986 European Library – Zaltbommel/Netherlands

No part of this book may be reproduced in any form, by print, photoprint, microfilm or any other means, without written permission from the publisher.

INTRODUCTION

The period in Teignmouth's past concentrated on in this book is 1880 to 1930. Although it is not primarily a work of history, the descriptions accompanying each illustration will, I hope, interest newcomers and young Teignmothians in the town's past and also bring back many memories for Teignmothians who knew the town before the Second World War.

Permanent photographic pictures on printing paper became possible only from 1840 and it is thanks to early photographers in Teignmouth such as Samuel Poole and George Denney that photographic records of the town survive from the 1850's onwards. By the time George Denney set himself up as a photographic artist in the 1880's Britain was suffering an economic recession. A sign of the times in Teignmouth was the rebuilding of the Soup Kitchen in Willey Lane in 1887, but there was also a significant amount of other building during the decade that pointed to a mood of optimism about the town's future. Work started on quay extensions to improve harbour trade. A new market place and Town Hall (subsequently destroyed by bombs in the 1940's) replaced the market erected in 1820. Several new places of worship for nonconformists were built or rebuilt; a new post office was designed, public baths rebuilt, and a new railway station constructed. Trades in the 1880's included coopers, cab proprietors, coach builders, sail makers, blacksmiths, harness makers, blacking makers, gunsmiths, basket makers and two town criers.

Soon after the turn of the century a bowling green and tennis courts were laid down on the Den, but interest in theatre entertainment dwindled as the novelty of cinematograph pictures captured public imagination. The theatre at the Athenaeum in Gales Hill closed, leaving the pierrots on the small pavilion stage near The Point to fill the gap partially with music hall songs and turns. At home some families entertained themselves with their own private theatricals, and gathering round the family piano passed many an hour in the evening. Teignmouth had two pianoforte warehouses (at 2 and 9 Somerset Place) from which pianos were hired as well as sold. Home entertainment was often a matter of possessing some skill at a particular craft, perhaps woodcarving, needlework or sketching, all done by gaslight. There was a School of Art in Orchard Gardens from 1885 until 1910 which gave technical instruction and craft lessons along with courses in the higher arts. Families were larger then and often ten children or more would settle round the hearth to listen to the Bible or a work of literature being read out aloud. Many local people will remember Morton Woolley's shop at 3 Bank Street (now Currys) where the British & Foreign Bible Society and the Religious Tract Society had depots and a reading room.

The Great War brought mixed fortunes for trades in Teignmouth as men left for the front, and the town's usual visitors had their own wartime priorities elsewhere. Many businesses did not survive. As the war years went on food shortages (bread, tea, potatoes, sugar) made the already uncertain times worse, and many families found their lives tragically disrupted: over 175 Teignmouth men made the supreme sacrifice.

Those grim times were not without the wry local humour,

however. One publican tried as hard as he knew to gain exemption from military service but was refused since brewing beer was not considered of national importance. He pointed out that it helped the revenue but was told by the Tribunal: 'That may be so but we don't look at it from that point of view.'

In the 1920's there was work to do to stimulate the town's economy but people also wanted some enjoyment. The new golf course on Little Haldon was opened; Morgan Giles established his shipyard business on the Strand; and the motorised char-à-banc took employees and their families on annual outings. When the lively charleston dance came to town eyebrows were raised along with hemlines.

By 1930 Teignmouth was on the verge of a new age. Transport since the 1880's had undergone a transformation, and for a while the new ways of getting to different places meant that Teignmouth remained as popular as ever with visitors of comfortable means. In a 1930 guide book Teignmouth is promoted as the only south coast resort offering complete aviation facilities: instruction, air taxis, aeroplane overhauls and joy riding daily at the Haldon Aerodrome & School of Flying. But the horse carriage of the 1880's had lost ground to the motor car and omnibus, and soon people less prosperous would be the town's main visitors. By then the old trades such as sailmaking and coachbuilding had been extinguished along with the street gaslamps, but if a Teignmothian from Victorian or Edwardian times was asked what had most changed in the town's appearance he or she would point to the roads and traffic.

In the 1880's some of the town's streets were described as narrow and ill-paved – but free from double yellow lines and the intrusive motor car they must also have been a shopper's delight.

As Shaldon celebrates its Georgian days and Totnes its Elizabethan days, it is appropriate to reflect on how Teignmouth might salute and thrive on the best of its Victorian past, and with that thought in mind I hope readers will enjoy looking at each photograph as much as I have enjoyed becoming better acquainted with Teignmouth's past.

Ann Pearson

Acknowledgements

L.B. Birch, May Bovey, Mrs. E. Bowyer, Cyril Boyne, Mrs. Causley, Mr. and Mrs. G.K. Collyer, Ken Cook, George Day, Kathleen Ellis, Christine Gribble, Mrs. C. Martin, Russell Merrifield, Philip Nathan, Miss C.B. Nepean, Ada Norsworthy, Mavis Piller, Joan Powell, Dorothy Spencer, Teignbridge District Council (Councillor P.C. Riggs), Teignmouth Museum and Historical Society (Mollie Weare and John Reed), Teignmouth Town Council (Councillor Peter Winterbottom and Jim Gresham, Town Clerk), Margaret Wearn and Philip Winchester.

44165. TEIGNMOUTH. FROM THE PIER.

1. Brightly painted bathing machines, tea kiosks, bonnets, straw boaters and parasols epitomise a seaside holiday in Teignmouth before the Great War. There were donkey and pony rides, and Mr. Harrison's pierrots towards The Point. Emma Dodd ran a cockle stall selling a 1d. plate of cockles or 1½d. worth of winkles, and the ice cream was sold by Antonucci from Teign Street. They were also fried potato and fried fish dealers. An ice cream cornet cost ½d. For a penny you could have a wafer, and 1½d. would buy a wafer with sugar biscuit. For a few shillings the visitor could enjoy carriage drives or steamer excursions from the Pier, and so that their presence in town might be proclaimed visitors could record their names in a Visitors' Book kept at 'The Teignmouth Gazette' printing works in Station Road. Some visitors then took apartments or a whole house for a stay of several weeks or months, often bringing servants with them.

2. The pavilion near The Point (upper right) is where the pierrots and vaudeville acts entertained the public. Two of the comics employed by Mr. Harrison were Wally Beadle and Sid Vernon (later a postman in Dawlish). The performances were screened off and some youngsters climbed up a pillar to sneak a free glimpse of the entertainment. Only one child at a time could watch from the pillar and so turns were taken to climb up and report to the others what was happening on the small stage. The pierrots fascinated everyone, with their whitened faces and baggy white costumes but it was not so much the acts and songs that drew the children as the chance of getting a forbidden peep.

3. This photograph showing one of the earliest types of bathing machine dates from about 1885. Even then bathing machines had existed for over a hundred years. The hood at the front allowed an extra bit of modesty when the bather stepped from the machine into the water. The man on the right is believed to be the pier master and bathing machine proprietor, George English, as a young man. He would say, 'Duck ladies, duck your bumsies' as he helped his customers step down. Children knew the lady on the left as Aunty Betsworth who taught them swimming, and here she appears to be changing the towels supplied inside the machines. Bathing dresses could also be hired. Notice the shrimping net on the left, and also the four ornamental pagodas at the entrance to the pier, which were later incorporated into one large covered entrance surrounded by advertisement hoardings.

4. Bewildered residents survey the disaster which struck Teignmouth Pier and sea front in January 1908. During the night a strong easterly wind and high tide undermined the supports of the Pier, leaving several of them hanging. The tide also removed thousands of tons of sand and shingle and badly damaged both ends of the promenade. More damage followed within hours. The following morning's tide backed by the full force of the east wind whiplashed the Pier foundations and eventually the shore end of the Pier collapsed, taking with it the pavilion and shop shown here resting at an angle of 45°. Several feet of the promenade crashed with it.

5. In a guide book from the 1890's two of the pagodas shown in the background of plate 3 were mentioned as being at the entrance of the Pier, and one of them can be seen quite clearly in the photograph of the 1908 storm damage. £15,000 was spent on making good the damage caused to the sea front, extending the promenade and constructing a lower promenade, but the pagodas were replaced by small pyramid-type structures. Notice the man in the trench coat and the boy in the tunic suit who make sure they get themselves recorded in both photographs of the memorable event, in exactly the same way as modern spectators whose heads bob in and out of television newsreels.

Pier Promenade, Teignmouth.

6. This postcard from about 1900 shows the iron archway from which lanterns lit the Pier in the evenings. Bench seating ran the full length of the Pier promenade on both sides, and promenaders could relax to the sounds of water lapping underneath and the melodies of live music wafting through the sea air. Open-air concerts were held on The Den every day in the summer, and an orchestra played twice daily on the Pier. Small shelters along the promenade allowed ladies an additional place in which to shield their skin from the sun and wind. It was not fashionable then for delicate ladies to acquire a sun tan so their packing cases for the seaside included large sun hats and parasols. Those who worked the land or waters had no such restrictions and thought the pale visitors an unhealthy lot.

7. 'Magic Lantern' shows with magnified images changing in succession to create the illusion of movement were very popular. Here a crowd of 300 or so early cinema-goers pose to have their picture taken in 1911 at the entrance to the Pier, which advertises 'Pictures Tonight'. By that time they may have been moving picture films. Look at the glum face of the little boy in the middle of the front row, firmly held by his mother: he looks fed up with waiting to get into the show! In those days there would have been a notice in theatre halls asking ladies to remove their hats during performances, and it is easy to see why. Notice also all the advertisements of local firms: The London Hotel, May & Son of Somerset Place, Mr. Evans' Medical Hall on the corner of Orchard Gardens and Fore Street, and Southwoods of Northumberland Place.

8. Before the Great War the Den was developed by providing sporting facilities for summer entertainment. Teignmouth had its first season of bowls in 1909 when the bowling green was opened and a committee formed to arrange fixtures. The charge for a game was 2d. per hour. Spectators watched from canopied seats set into the bank, just visible on the right-hand side and foreground of this postcard, and while their parents relaxed children could play hopscotch on squares painted on the path by the seats. Before the present bowls pavilion was built there was a hut by the green used as a cookhouse by Americans garrisoned in Teignmouth during the Second World War. Note the ivy-encrusted Courtenay house in the centre, once the summer home of the Courtenay family, Earls of Devon, who owned the Den. They had a clear view over it of another summer house across the river, Ness House owned by the Cliffords, lords of the manor in west Teignmouth.

9. As well as bowls the Den was ideal for another popular sport, the Teignmouth Bicycle Races which drew competitors from a national field and a large number of spectators to witness the events, along with numerous officials: handicappers, lap scorers, a timekeeper, starter and clerk of the course. In 1880 there were five races. The 1-mile Handicap Race attracted club competitors from Ilminster, Edinburgh University, Clifton, Bristol and Plymouth. There was also a 3-mile Town Race, a 5-mile Grand Challenge Race, open to members of any recognised bicycle club, a 2-mile Open Handicap Race for which a silver cup was awarded by the licensed victuallers, and a 1-mile Consolation Race with a silver-plated bicycle horn as first prize. All this was only a few years after the penny-farthing bicycle became popular (in the early 1870's) and the development of the modern bicycle in 1876. The new craze caught on quickly, and I regret there was no more suitable photograph to show the enthusiasm. The Teignmouth Rovers Club had their headquarters at the London Hotel.

The Tennis Courts, Teignmouth.

10. For ladies, playing tennis in a long skirt was easier than cycling, always assuming they were willing to dispense with wearing the customary corset. Lady cycling enthusiasts were somewhat hampered by their long dresses until a London clothier invented a safety cycling skirt for comfort in riding. There was an advertisement claim in a book on Teignmouth published in 1901 that a new type of corset possessed an unbreakable waist and natural hinge 'so that the wearer does not break the steels when stooping'. Curiously, only the men seem to be moving in this tennis match photographed after the Great War. The tennis courts were laid down in 1910 and in the early 1920's the charge for a game was 3s. per court per hour in the main summer months, which seems rather expensive.

11. This floral carpet roll photographed on the promenade in 1913 no doubt attracted many admirers. What a pity we can see it in black and white only. The keeping of the Den and other pleasure grounds was put out to tender by the old Teignmouth Board in the 1880's, as was scavenging, removing refuse and repairing roads. Changes came after the new Teignmouth Urban District Council was formed in 1894. An advertisement in 1902 offered the handsome salary of £175 per annum for a surveyor to manage public grounds. The Council's General Foreman and Storekeeper received just 35s. (£1.75) per week.

The Cemetery, Teignmouth.

12. If this seems a strange photograph to include, it may seem even more strange that it was used as a postcard in 1910 by someone who had visited the cemetery as part of his morning's walk. In the days before common ownership of the telephone the quickest and cheapest form of sending messages to friends and relatives was by postcard (the cost of postage was ½d.) and since Teignmouth residents might want to send cards to the same relative each week a wide selection was needed to avoid duplication presumably. Management of the cemetery, which opened in 1856, was one of the many duties of the Council surveyor. He received an extra £5 per annum as Surveyor to the Burial Board.

Floral Tide Clock, Teignmouth.

13. Like the floral carpet roll, this floral tide clock photographed at the turn of the century is an example of the considerable skill of council gardeners. It gave an additional dab of bright colour to promenaders and rich visitors staying in suites at The Royal Hotel opposite. The Royal was then the most fashionable place to stay in town, able to boast that it had 'enjoyed the patronage of our own Royal, and Continental Royal Families, and of the Aristocracy of the Kingdom'. Full board at the hotel was over ten shillings per day before the Great War and although service was thoroughly reliable, it seems the tide clock was not. After the war there was another tide clock nearer to the lighthouse, and some residents now confess to resetting the hands as a prank!

Den Road, Teignmouth.

14. The best known clock in town was, and still is, Rossiter's drum clock in Den Road. This view was almost certainly photographed in 1909 since the drum clock is missing from its hinges: early in that year it was removed and replaced at a cost of almost £100, the first drum clock erected in the 1880's having given 25 years of service. To provide such a clock was a generous act of public service by George Rossiter in the days before all people carried their own timepieces. Usually only public buildings such as churches or town halls provided clocks. Other points of interest are the cabbie's shelter opposite the post office and not least of all the fact that photographers with their very cumbersome plate cameras and tripods all those years ago could stand for several minutes in a spot which would surely now invite a nasty accident.

GENERAL POST OFFICE, TEIGNMOUTH

15. This photograph of Den Road before the Great War shows Rossiter's watchmaker's shop in the far right and next to it a fancy repository run by the Misses Jane and Ellen Stephens from the 1880's until the war. Next is the shop of William Hannaford & Son, nurserymen, and Henry Rice's drapery. In the days of labour intensive industry the main Post Office opened from 7 am to 9 pm on weekdays and from 7 am to 10 am on Sundays. Letters could be posted up to 8.40 pm for delivery to London and all parts. The photograph is interesting for its reminder of old road conditions in the main thoroughfares. Note the two paved crossings set into the road, which allowed pedestrians to cross without muddying boots or long dresses in the days before roads were properly surfaced. Potholes left by horses and carriages, plus horse dung, must have been real hazards for daydreamers.

16. The architecture of Den Road looking towards Orchard Gardens has changed hardly at all. Lucy's Library on the corner of Wellington Street has been rebuilt with a classical balustrade around a flat roof for the Midland Bank, but otherwise only the transport of the day – around 1900 – sets it in another age. Seth Mitchell who ran the refreshment rooms on the corner of Brunswick Street (on the left) later became a carriage proprietor in Northumberland Place but the premises continued to be run as a restaurant for many years. The Liberal Club had their premises above the restaurant (4 Den Road) before moving to Exeter Street and then the Market Inn in Brunswick Street in the 1930's. Members enjoyed 'smoking concerts' in the Club's reading room, with piano and violin accompaniments. It is difficult to fit modern traffic lights and a pedestrian crossing into this tree-lined gas-lit street of 85 years ago.

17. All the flags and bunting were brought out to adorn Teignmouth's streets for King George V's Coronation in 1911, and residents who were willing to decorate their homes for the occasion by putting up outside illuminations in the evening were allowed the cost of gas free. Bellringers of the two Anglican churches received £2 10s. 0d. for each church to ring out the happy celebrations, and a great procession of bands, youth organisations, military units and members of prominent local services made their way round the town. In this photograph they are in Orchard Gardens. To mark the occasion the Council gave workmen a two-day paid holiday plus a bonus of 2s. 6d., and children were treated to a Coronation tea and Coronation medal.

Teignmouth. Orchard Gardens. 10072

18. At 4 Orchard Gardens (behind the man walking in the road) a Temperance Hall was established in 1879. Local papers carried frequent reports of public drunkenness, women as well as men, and the cause of temperance was dear to the hearts of the Misses Caroline and Emily Fry who ran the Hall for almost 50 years. Fear of a national drinking problem prompted various religious groups to support teetotal campaigns and mass pledges, and evangelical lectures were held in the Hall warning of the dangers of excessive drinking. Temperance societies and hotels (there was a Temperance Hotel in Station Road) tried to keep the drink habit from spreading. The Hall became the regular meeting place of the Church of England Temperance Society on Tuesday nights and the Saturday afternoon Band of Hope for children, though the Hall was also used for scientific lectures, concerts and magic lantern shows. Miss Alice Roberts carried on the temperance work of the Misses Fry but the Hall was eventually sold in 1938.

19. Several of Teignmouth's 28 licensed premises in this postcard from the 1920's have now gone, and even with the help of many local people it has proved impossible to identify all of them with certainty, especially as each picture is so small. The ones that can be named are given from the left, from top to bottom, and the street is mentioned in brackets for those that no longer exist: Custom House Inn (Old Quay), Lifeboat Inn, Blue Anchor, Beehive (Bitton Street), Sebastopol (Myrtle Hill), Ship Inn, Jolly Sailor, ? (possibly the Market Inn in Brunswick Street), Old Quay Inn (demolished February 1985), Bird in Hand (Lower Brook Street), Devon Arms, Royal Hotel, New Quay Inn, Royal Oak (Commercial Road), London Hotel, Railway Hotel (Station Road), Prince of Wales (Fore Street), Teign Brewery, Beach Hotel, Half Moon, King William IV Inn, Black Horse (Bitton Road), ?, Dawlish Inn, Golden Lion, Kings Arms, ?, ?

20. This aerial photograph of Orchard Gardens taken around 1930 gives a most interesting reminder of the houses and streets behind, all gone and now the site of a large car park and inner ring road. The large wall in the upper left of the picture is the railway cutting. Many local people will have fond memories of the Bird in Hand pub in Lower Brook Street, the White Hart in Higher Brook Street and the Victory working men's club, but perhaps not so fond memories in some cases of Brook Street School (right of centre). Some girls there in the late 1920's say they were terrified by Miss Kitty Sharam, Assistant Mistress, who was always very strict in demanding punctuality and obedience. The school was established in 1879, a year before attendance was made compulsory throughout the land.

21. St. James' Church was rebuilt in 1820/21 and this rare photograph from the 1880's shows the church before the choir vestry was erected in 1893 (to the right of the yew tree). The gas lantern arch over the gateway has gone though part of one metal section still remains embedded in the left-hand pillar, and the rendering has been removed from the wall to reveal the original red sandstone construction. Also notice the cobbled pavement on the right and the wheel grooves in the unmade road. Council water carts (see plate 16) watered roads to keep dust down but the sloping roads here were a favourite place with errand boys who used to ride their wheelbarrows down the hills as furiously as they could and churn up the surface in the process. Their only fear during the perilous joyride was being spotted by a policeman.

22. This studio photograph taken after the Great War shows Mrs. Ada Norsworthy (née Betsworth) in Girl Guide uniform. On her belt she carried a knife and whistle, and the tie doubled as an emergency sling. When a guide became an officer the felt hat where the brim turns up was decorated with a cockade to denote rank. The Girl Guide movement came to Teignmouth in 1911 when the first patrol was formed by Miss Lois Liptrott, daughter of the vicar of St. James' Church, and many of the skills learned by the girls were a useful reserve during the Great War. Teamwork and team spirit are still important for today's Guides, though it is probable that the independence and self-confidence acquired by the earliest Guides played a part in convincing those in political authority that women should be allowed to vote in general elections. Many prominent townspeople were against female enfranchisement, however. Queen Victoria herself condemned the 'mad, wicked folly of Women's Rights'.

23. This is believed to be an interior view of the old Teignmouth Hospital in Dawlish Road, and is another example of the unusual photographs once mass produced for postcards. The patient in bed on the left looks too ill to protest! The hospital was immediately next to the United Reformed Church on the west side, before the town's main hospital was transferred to Mill Lane in the 1920's. There was also a small hospital at Lower Bitton for infectious diseases. At one time this was housed temporarily in Willow Street but had to be moved following complaints from anxious neighbours. Early in 1880 there was a report of a boy suffering from measles being removed from a vessel in the harbour to the infectious diseases hospital, causing some concern about the means of transport for such patients. This was always by ordinary cab which 'however carefully they might afterwards be disinfected, was very undesirable' said the Medical Officer. He pressed for an ambulance to be purchased.

24. Wounded soldiers of the Great War pose cheerfully to have their photograph taken outside the old Teignmouth Hospital. Note the man in his slippers second from left in the front row. Frostbite affecting both feet was not uncommon during long months in the trenches. Although food shortages increased as the war went on, the hospital received weekly gifts of food from wellwishers, as well as books, bandages, medicine bottles, socks, cigarettes, linen and walking sticks. The government urged everyone to grow more vegetables, and amongst the many new allotments that were needed even the lawn of the council school was dug up for planting potatoes, and the public were urged to use substitutes for potatoes, sugar and tea. Despite everything the welfare of the troops remained paramount. A Canteen and Recreation Hall was opened for them at the Town Hall and regular concerts were held in the town for their entertainment.

Teignmouth, Bilton Park.

25. Bitton House also saw use as a hospital, and many will remember the Isolation Hospital at Lower Bitton built by the UDC in 1905. Bitton Park, shown here before the Great War, does not look much different today now that the Orangery has been restored. The mature trees encircled by bench seats on the left and the two trees in front of Bitton House have all gone, giving the house a more open prospect. The size of the grounds has always made them an obvious place for public events, and one of the more unusual used to be archery which became popular in the 1850's. For the next two or three decades the park was used regularly for grand archery fetes with competitions and prizes for men's and ladies' events. Tending to such a large area of grass was a job calling literally for considerable horse power: a cart horse was once used to pull the large cylinder mowers.

CAPT. MORRISON - BELL.

26. Bitton Park was closed to the public for much of the Great War during the occupation of Bitton House by military authorities but before the war Teignmouth's Member of Parliament, Captain Ernest Fitzroy Morrison-Bell (later Colonel), presided over a summer tea given by the Council in the grounds to French journalists. He was M.P. for the old Mid-Devon Constituency from 1908 to 1918. Changes in parliamentary boundaries meant there was an unwelcome prospect of Teignmouth going into the new Torquay division in 1918 but Col. Morrison-Bell petitioned Parliament successfully in getting Teignmouth transferred to the more acceptable Totnes division. Amongst other measures for the town, he supported a bill enabling health and seaside resorts to spend money out of rates in advertising, one of the major steps in the modern tourist industry. His brother, Sir Arthur Clive Morrison-Bell, was M.P. for the Honiton divison.

The Tennis Ground, Teignmouth.

27. An open field has replaced the tennis court at Lower Bitton, and the land beyond is the Rugby Football ground. On the other side of the railway line the top shoreground has become the Polly Steps car park and launching slipway. This is how the Bitton estate looked at the turn of the century soon after it ceased to be privately owned. Bitton House was not used as Council offices until 1928 but the estate played a part in celebrating the opening of the new Town Hall in Brunswick Street in 1883. Mrs. Parson who then owned the Bitton estate gave permission for a grand procession to assemble in the grounds to mark the inauguration of Teignmouth Board's new offices, Market and Baths. Several bands, the Oddfellows, Volunteer Artillery, Rifle Volunteers and officials in horse-drawn carriages gathered here to parade through streets lined with cheering crowds, and schoolchildren marched with the St. James's Drum & Fife Band to the Den where they were treated to a sumptuous tea.

28. Many of these faces from Teignmouth's rugby football team in 1927/28 will be familiar to Teignmothians. The photograph, taken outside Bitton House, was kindly loaned by Philip Nathan (seated second from left in the middle row). He played football until the age of 45, spent nearly thirty years as a 'special' in the police force and used to act as Teignmouth's town crier on special occasions. Frank Davey (standing 9th from left in the back row) had the distinction of playing for England, although never played for Devon.

Teignmouth Harbour.

29. The western quay and storage sheds shown here after completion in 1893 marked a considerable improvement in the harbour's fortunes, opening up safe berths for shipping. Dock sites were let out to several companies dealing in cereals, building materials, coal and manure. The traditional loading methods of sailing ships on deep water moorings midstream however, continued into the 1930's. Not all shipowners were willing to pay the extra harbour dues for using the improved quays. Nevertheless the improvements brought a significant increase in trade, and larger vessels were able to use the port instead of taking their cargoes elsewhere. Steamships plied one side of the docks and steam trains the other side.

30. Work began on the western quay extensions in 1888. Before that the Old Quay on the left with its railway siding and the New Quay on the far right were the harbour's two main quays. Water round the New Quay, built in the 1820's, was deeper then and vessels were also able to use the Shaldon side of the harbour. The large three-gabled building on the Old Quay was once used by Pickfords as a store but was originally built to house French prisoners during the Napoleonic Wars. It was also used for storing codfish during the height of the Newfoundland trade. In the 1950's the roof was badly burned in a fire. Apart from the railway, this is very much how Teignmouth harbour would have appeared to the marine artist, Thomas Luny, who painted so many scenes of it in the early years of the nineteenth century.

31. James Finch, coal merchant and ship owner, purchased the New Quay from the Earl of Devon in the mid-1890's and built storage and office accommodation on the quay. Previously there was a clear view of the New Quay Inn along the back beach. Note the rows of washing hanging out to dry along the beach, a working beach which in those days was not usually frequented by the town's visitors. The boathouses behind then housed boats on the ground floor (now converted to lounges) with living accommodation above. Along the beach were a series of large timbers used as mooring posts (several still remain) to which the leaning vessel is secured. Since there was no dry dock ships were brought as far as possible up the beach for ship bottoms to be scraped and tarred.

32. This similar view of the back beach photographed before 1893 shows the New Quay before the quay buildings were erected. Then, as now, most of the boatowners in town lived in the river frontage streets but in those days there were several boat builders too. The boatyard in The Strand was owned by the Teignmouth Ship & Yacht Company before being taken over by Gann & Palmer, but most people will remember it as Morgan Giles' Shipyard from the 1920's to the 1960's. Many prestigious, hand-built vessels went down the slipway on this beach, varying from simple rowing boats to luxurious racing yachts and minesweepers for the Admiralty. In the nineteenth century large merchant ships built by Mansfield's company also launched from a slipway here, including a 700-ton ship named 'Crystal Palace' for the Great Exhibition in 1851.

33. These are some of the men whose expertise as shipwrights, joiners, engineers and other trades brought international renown to Teignmouth as a place of shipbuilding excellence at the Morgan Giles Shipyard. Pictured in about 1929, Mr. F.C. Morgan Giles is on the far right. 1. Frank Luscombe, 2. Charlie Young, 3. Bert Tucker, 4. Bill Howard, 5. Jack Back, 6. Ron Churchill, 7. Fred Scagell, 8. George Cummings, 9. Bill Foot, 10. ? Collins, 11. Reg Yeabsley, 12. Jimmy Wild, 13. Cecil Wise, 14. Bill Lambert ('Wire'!), 15. Bill Moor, 16. Percy Woodgates, 17. Bert Banham, 18. Gordon Colbran, 19. Fred Babbage, 20. Louis Barrett ('Chiefie'), 21. Lloyd Foot and 22. F.C. Morgan Giles.

34. This snapshot taken in 1927 shows the Morgan Giles Shipyard from the estuary, and also Mr. G.K. Collyer and Reg Yeabsley sailing a national class 14' dinghy. Mr. Collyer, who went to the yard as a boy and rose to be chief draughtsman and a director, recently compiled a history of the shipyard to commemorate its contribution to the town and the high standard of workmanship carried on there. Hopefully even more traces of the ancient craft of shipbuilding carried on in Teignmouth over many centuries will be uncovered when building developers start work on the site. Teignmouth was one of the major westcountry ports liable to have ships and men requisitioned by monarchs during wars, and it is certain that ships from here saw action in such famous campaigns as the defeat of the Spanish Armada.

35. There are several photographs of the second Alfred Staniforth lifeboat presented to the town in 1896, but this rare photograph dates from before then and is either of the first Alfred Staniforth boat or, more likely, the second Arnold lifeboat which was in service in the early 1890's. The first Alfred Staniforth boat was given in 1894 but proved unsuitable and had to be returned to London only a few months later. Note the stone front of the lifeboat house and the decorative brickwork above the RNLI sign, now hidden by modern rendering. Trying to row a lifeboat over the sand bar in heavy seas was in itself a courageous achievement. At times the lifeboat would be completely concealed by immense waves, and not until the bar was cleared could the sails be hoisted and distressed victims reached.

36. In the days before push-button entertainment Lifeboat Day was a local festival attracting large crowds. Once on its carriage, the lifeboat was hauled through town by a team of horses. Spectators lined every vantage point along the sea front and pier. The carriage tracks can be seen in the sand where the lifeboat has been hauled towards the pier for launching. Note the shadows cast by strong sunlight and the fashionable parasol held by the lady in the carriage. The photograph dates from the turn of the century when class differences were very pronounced. Those of high status would send servants into Teignmouth shops to ask shopkeepers to bring goods out for display so that a selection could be made without the customer troubling to step down from his or her carriage. Only if it was raining would a shop owner dare refuse.

LAUNCHING THE LIFEBOAT AT TEIGNMOUTH.

37. Lifeboat Day was most of all a proud occasion for the crew, giving them a chance to show off their gleaming boat and their own nautical skills. The boat was deliberately capsized to demonstrate its self-righting ability. Someone would climb up the mast and over the boat would go with the crew and as it came upright the men would stand to loud cheers and applause from the crowd. Some will tell you they were even dry as they stood up! Of course much of the pride (and occasional tall story) was due to the town having its own lifeboat and local crew. The second Alfred Staniforth shown here served Teignmouth until 1931. By the time Teignmouth's last lifeboat, the Henry Finlay, ceased service in 1940 the number of lives saved by Teignmouth men over the years totalled over 125.

38. The Lifeboat sometimes attended water polo matches, as in this 1904 event. Water polo matches played on Saturday afternoons or evenings off the pier were a big attraction, and the sight of acetylene flares lighting some of the evening matches added to the sense of excitement. The swimmers' changing room was on the pier and a club members' card had to be produced at the turnstile to avoid paying the 2d. entrance fee to the pier. Once changed the swimmers dropped on to the beach by means of a ladder from a trapdoor near the beach end of the pier. Some of the more spirited boys who could join the swimming club from the age of 12 hoped to amuse themselves by startling anyone on the beach below as they dropped down from the trapdoor.

39. The water polo matches were organised by the Teignmouth Swimming & Lifesaving Society who did much to promote the art of swimming. Swimming from the Parson & Clerk rocks to Hackney and other such distances was a strenuous test of stamina which shows the high standard reached by members. The senior water polo team for 1905 included Billy Rowe (sitting 3rd on right) and Harry Smith (centre, sitting on the lower step of the bathing machine), both of whom would occasionally swim from the pier to Babbacombe. Sitting on the left in the front row is Puggy Milton and behind him is Welham. Perhaps some readers will know the other three. Members of the Teignmouth team were champions of Devon for many years, and fixtures were arranged with the most important teams in England and Wales. A 1925 guide book to the town says: *Their fame at this most exciting and strenuous game has reached all over the country and they have met and generally defeated such well-known sides as Wigan, Weston-super-Mare, Hyde Seal, Ashton, Surrey Ramblers, London City Police and many other famous teams.*

40. Regatta Day, pictured here before the Great War, is a great occasion known to Teignmothians for something like 200 years, the sailing and rowing matches once attracting the nobility and gentry. The fun fair on the Den now has its own separate week in the summer, but the sounds and sights of a modern fair are rather different. George Denney who took this photograph and who was also Honorary Secretary of the Regatta Committee would have heard gypsy fiddlers, steam organs and harmonium players who attracted small crowds on their own account. The roundabouts were also steam-driven, and some of the sideshows then were boxing booths, jugglers and fortune tellers. Note the pleasure steamer alongside the end of the pier. Annual Regattas in Teignmouth are believed to be amongst the earliest established on the south coast, but no doubt gatherings for boat races have a more ancient origin than 200 years.

41. The Den when empty of crowds for special occasions and the promenade still retain their attractions for early morning walkers. With their view over the bay, the fashionable buildings were favoured venues for exclusive clubs. The East Devon & Teignmouth Club occupied what is now the Riviera Cinema and there was also the South View Club (left of the Royal Hotel, just out of view) established in 1902 as a non-political club with rooms for billiards, reading, smoking and cards. Many people will remember the sea front when it looked like this at the turn of the century. It hardly changed at all for several more decades. Now several buildings block all but a tiny glimpse of the Den, and the formal gardens of Courtenay Place have become small car parks. The photograph was taken from Esplanade house bombed during the Second World War and now the site of a roundabout.

Den House Private Hotel - Teignmouth.

42. Den House (Bella Vista holiday flats) has altered very little from the photograph taken of it in the late 1920's when the proprietors were the Misses Beetlestone. All the decorative ironwork remains but the wall in front has gone, and a buttery bar has been opened on the left-hand side. Touring by car became fashionable in the flamboyant twenties but the hotel's sign indicates that motorists were still a rare breed. Interestingly, breeding of the refined kind played an important part in a former use of Den House: in the 1820's it was an academy for ladies, one of five such academies in Teignmouth at that time.

43. St. Michael's Church was rebuilt in 1822-23 but the old tower did not enhance its appearance, and in 1887 work began on the present taller tower built in the more ornate Gothic style in celebration of Queen Victoria's Jubilee. A new chancel was built in 1875 followed by new seating in 1882, a new vestry and font in 1885, a peal of bells and clock chimes in the 1890's and a restored and enlarged organ. Such prolific refurbishing work is a mark of the Victorian enthusiasm for building or rebuilding new places of worship, along with the many other public buildings deemed necessary by the interest in modern town planning. Hardly a decade passed without a new church appearing in Teignmouth, partly encouraged by the rivalry between high church/low church and conformist/nonconformist and the felt need to give a public display of one's preferences, which is a reminder of the biblical language and sentiments commonplace to Victorian Teignmothians throughout the home, school and public life.

44. Just past St. Michael's elegant town houses look over the promenade towards the pier. Only recently their use has changed to private flats (formerly Bairnscroft Hotel) but this is how they appeared before the Great War. Note the garden wall on the right made of old red sandstone, the local building rock which lies behind many of the masonry facings of Teignmouth's prominent buildings. Older Teignmothians may recall George Denney, the photographer, who lived in the Clifton boarding house on the left. As well as his associations with the Regatta Committee, he was on the bowling green and lawn tennis committees and a member of the Urban District Council for 12 years until 1917.

45. There are probably many of George Denney's photographs still gracing Teignmouth homes and family albums. He established his photographic business in the 1880's in a promenade studio at East Cliff in front of the houses in plate 44. Ordinary families in the first half of the nineteenth century were lucky if one of them was talented enough to be able to record their likenesses in a sketch, but by the second half of the century instant portraiture for all became possible, transforming Victorian mantelpieces and walls. Eventually the skills in studio photography could be practised in the open air, and by the turn of the century photography was well established as a hobby. Visitors to the town started to bring amateur camera equipment with them on holiday, and the larger hotels included a photographer's dark room amongst facilities offered to guests.

46. Visitors without their own camera could have a record of their stay in Teignmouth in group photographs such as this one taken on the beach outside Denney's studio in about 1910. Although it took several minutes for the group to assemble the informality of the occasion makes it a fascinating study of Edwardian relaxation by the sea. Look at the young man holding the shoulders of his fiancée or wife, the wooden toy spade held by the girl at the front and the very shy-faced little girl on the right. Then there are the fashions: the crimped hair and parasols of the ladies and the men's round-collared shirts. Even though they are on the beach all the men and boys wear a tie, and suitable dress for the ladies means nothing showing below the neckline.

Jawbones of Whale. Teignmouth.

47. The pairs of whale jawbones at each end of the raised promenade are amongst the best known of old Teignmouth's landmarks. Presented to the town by Pike Ward who engaged in the Icelandic whaling industry, the jawbones gradually deteriorated and had to be removed a few years after the Second World War when they became unsafe. Notice the beautifully ornate ironwork of the gas lampstand on the left-hand stone pillar, and also the lady with parasol sitting in the bathchair. Bathchairs as well as deck chairs were available for hire. The card is postmarked August 1913, and in the quaint language of the time the writer tells her friend back home in Birmingham: *Having a ripping time; like the place, A.l. Just going on the steamer to Torquay.*

SEA WALL, TEIGNMOUTH.

48. Before the whale jawbones appeared as an extra novelty, the main marvel by the sea wall was a train from the steam age puffing its way majestically along the coastal track, a familiar sight for over a hundred years. All photographers still hope a train will appear in the camera lens at the right time. None of the Edwardians snapped here, however, seems particularly pleased to find a photographer blocking the path. Note the 'Jimmy Edwards' character on the right giving a suspicious sideways glance. The lad in charge of the pony and invalid chair is Walter Nathan, Philip's older brother. The small shelters on the raised promenade gave way in the 1930's to a large pavilion built in celebration of King George V's Silver Jubilee.

49. Sprey Point is instantly recognisable but the Halfway Café photographed in the 1920's with its well-laid out lawns, tables and chairs had gone by the time of the Second World War. What a good use it was of this small promontory and a welcome sight to visitors after a long train journey. Many people recall the enjoyment of al fresco refreshments after a stroll along the sea wall walk, and watching the distant lights of shipping in the bay at dusk while sipping coffee. The café was not connected to the mains water supply so water had to be hauled in daily on a two-wheeled vehicle carrying a dustbin-sized drum. Steaming past is a 'King' class locomotive of the Great Western Railway.

Teignmouth, Smugglers' Lane.

50. It is no longer possible to launch a boat straight on to the water from Smugglers Lane, as it was when this photograph was taken in about 1906, since a stone wall now extends from the path across the water's edge. Note the small boat on the right of the tunnel-cum-boathouse which now has a modern toilet block built alongside. How ancient the lane is cannot be pinpointed but when it acquired its name centuries ago it was much more secluded. Any smugglers active in the mid-nineteenth century after the railway was built must have been dismayed by the number of exploring walkers brought to the cove as a result of the new sea wall. Construction work at Hole Head for the railway in 1846 also destroyed a smugglers' cave, perhaps the last straw for smugglers landing contraband here. Who knows…?

51. Halfway down Smugglers Lane from Holcombe there used to be a footbridge. All that remains to show where it crossed is a posthole and plinth on a wall above the brick building (converted to a garage). The neat fence on the right is still there in places but many posts have rotted, and the lane now has a tarmac surface though these are small details and Smugglers Lane would appear relatively unchanged to the small group out for a walk, perhaps a governess with children from one of the large private residences nearby. Note the coat of arms – a saltire between four fleurs de lis – which were represented on the portreeve's staff of office for west Teignmouth, and officially adopted as the town's arms in the last century.

52. Unfortunately the photographer of this view of Hole Head is unknown but its historic value will be appreciated by railway enthusiasts since it shows the single rail track which existed before this secton of the line was doubled in 1884. This is the old broad gauge (7' ¼") built by the South Devon Railway Company. The Great Western Railway acquired the line in 1876 and although the track was doubled in broad gauge in 1884 the days of the broad gauge were numbered. On its lines elsewhere GWR had already by 1875 converted to the standard gauge (4' 8½") recommended for all railways, and in 1892 this section of track had to be lifted again to lay the standard gauge, or 'narrow' gauge as it was always called in South Devon. Also note the original SDR tunnel, later completely rebuilt in rectangular shape by GWR and considerably enlarged to take two tracks.

53. Teignmouth Railway Station was rebuilt in the mid-1880's and a short tunnel outside it was opened at the same time as the track was redoubled. Several houses, the first Roman Catholic Church and part of the old hospital building all had to be demolished to make way for the opening and widening of the line through the town, and road bridges were then built over the opened tunnels. Shown here is the station before 1884, then situated a few yards further east than the new station. The most fashionable hotels (The Royal, London, Queens) sent hotel porters and carriages to meet every train. GWR passengers enjoyed every comfort, able to obtain luncheon baskets from principal stations during their journey to Teignmouth. Hot or cold luncheon with a bottle of beer was 3s. and there were tea baskets containing a pot of tea or coffee, bread and butter, cake or bun costing 1s. for one person or 1s. 6d. for two.

54. Station Road, before the ring road separated it from the railway station, was the way most train passengers came into town, passing on their way the Printing & Publishing Works where an illustrated guide book to the town could be purchased. In the 1920's the Printing Works and Steam Laundry were owned by Sidney Croydon and joint annual outings were arranged for the staff. Try to imagine a speed limit of just 12 m.p.h. and going over bumps and craters on solid tyres. The Steam Laundry later amalgamated with the Millbay Laundry from Regent Street, taking over the premises used by the Printing Works, but the Printing Works site was subsequently rebuilt and occupied by Liptons and the Steam Laundry premises became part of Lloyds Bank Chambers, disappearing along with the silks and flannels that staff once cleaned. Carpets were also cleaned and demothed by DDT, described in an advertisement as 'one of the most outstanding scientific discoveries of the [Great] war' though now known to be harmful to humans as well as insects!

55. Station Road (No. 2) and Lower Brook Street was where Bartletts' haulage business operated from before moving to Quay Road, and this brand new steam lorry was acquired after the Great War. Sturdily built, the wagon gave good service for many years. Apart from the furniture dealers, Coleridges, at Nos. 5 and 6, the trades carried on in Station Road after the Great War were quite different from those there today. There were two butchers' shops, Daws at No. 20 and Wills at No. 8, two cab proprietors (Hoare and Parker), Hayman the builders whose father built Teignmouth's first Roman Catholic church, the Railway hotel at No. 1, a linen draper at No. 4 and a fishmonger at No. 9 (Mr. Arthurs). The Police Station was also in Station Road, manned after the Great War by a superintendent, a sergeant and four constables.

56. May Bovey (née Sibley) loaned this photograph of a char-à-banc outing from The Triangle in the 1920's. Until a few years ago she was licensee with her husband at The Golden Lion, and in this photograph she is the little girl on the far right in the large bonnet. With her on the back seat from left to right are her grandad, father, mother, baby cousin, aunt Edie and gran Leyman. This was an annual Co-op outing, probably to the Moors for the day, and all the others in the char-à-banc are friends and neighbours. She recalls a procession of 10 to 12 coaches on each outing (this one is numbered 7 on the windscreen) and says the worst place to travel was in one of the rear vehicles because of the dust thrown up by those in front. The only remedy was to wear a veil over the face for some protection.

57. In this photograph of The Triangle and Regent Street taken in the 1880's the old Teignmouth of gaslight, cobbled pavements and bow windows is striking in contrast with neon lighting and the many larger stores of national chains in Teignmouth today. Maynards at 13 Triangle Place was then owned by Frederick Haymes, a saddler and harness maker. Nearest to us on the right is 13 Regent Street (now the Job Centre) run by George Medland, grocer, pork butcher, bacon factor and poulterer. He also had a stall in the Brunswick Street market hall. The next bow-windowed shop (now The Fun Shop) was an ironmongers at the turn of the century, and Terry's Greengrocers now occupies the dwelling in between. After the Great War Mrs. Monk-Jones, the chemist, had No. 11 Regent Street (now Carol's Kitchen), and any letters from satisfied customers would be displayed as recommendations of her potions.

58. By the 1920's The Triangle cab stand showed the new form of motorised transport taking over from the horse and carriage, and the end came for the Spanish oak tree planted to commemorate Queen Victoria's accession to the throne in 1837. Its space was needed for the construction of public toilets. Cave was a bookseller and stationer, and Lennards, the boot and shoe makers, had the shop on the corner of Wellington Street (now TSB). During an air raid in the Second World War the shop windows were blown out and boots and shoes flung into the road. Note the change in architecture on the other side of Wellington Street compared with plate 57. A more elaborate building with turrets has replaced the plain building facing Regent Street (Barclays Bank).

59. Look closely at this photograph of The Triangle around 1900 and you will see the drinking fountain left of the restaurant behind the horses. It was donated to the town in 1885 by Mr. and Mrs. James Wills. Another tree was uprooted to make way for the fountain when it was moved to the little Triangle in 1918 where it still stands. Unfortunately it was always of interest to children who amused themselves by polluting the water with stones, glass, etc. and the fountain proved too costly to maintain. Just right of the tree there was a smaller ornamental fountain set into a small garden enclosed by the railings. Left of the restaurant there has been a clear view up to the sea front since the Esplanade building behind the fountain was demolished after bomb damage in the Second World War (it is the large building on the left in plate 1). Also interesting are the paved walkways over Station Road and Holland Road (see notes with plate 15).

60. Cornish's in Wellington Street around 1900 became Cornish-Hobart's shop later (now Millets). Edward Cornish was a printer and stationer who published the now defunct 'Teignmouth Times' every Friday in competition with the 'Post' and 'Gazette' which later amalgamated. He also sold and hired cycles, and gave cycling lessons. Opposite was a bookseller and stationer's shop (now the Midland Bank) where Frederick Lucy housed his reading library. In common with other booksellers and libraries in Teignmouth and throughout the land, Lucy's Library was connected to Mudie's whose name denoted a carefully vetted standard for library subscribers. C.E. Mudie, a fervent evangelist, was the London proprietor of a nationally renowned circulating library and as he might buy several hundred copies of a new book his favourable interest was vital to authors and publishers, but the power of his circulating library also meant that he was able to exercise a tyrannical hold over readers' morals. On the opposite side of the street the small gardens have given way to a widened pavement bordering shop fronts. George Player, the coal merchant and ship owner, had premises here, as well as in Teign Street and on the Old Quay.

61. Until the recent construction of improved sea defence works, floods like this one in the 1920's were frequent in the town centre. The danger was not so much the sea as a combination of very heavy rain with an exceptional high tide which flooded the drains. When the streets were blocked like this there was nothing for it but to get out a rowing boat to do the shopping. If the extent of the flooding was very bad some youngsters found to their great delight that it was possible to row from one end of the town to the other almost without interruption. Notice the gas lamp standard on the right, disused after the arrival of electric street lighting. Just in front of the right-hand face of Rossiter's clock you may be able to make out one of the cup-shaped bulbs of the first electric street lights. Olivers, the sign above 10 Bank Street, was a bootmaker's shop, and Dring's, the chemist, is on the left in Wellington Street.

Carlton Terrace, Teignmouth.

62. For those who preferred not to swim in the sea there were hot and cold public baths and a large swimming bath built in Carlton Place in 1883, just out of this picture on the left. Only one of the houses in this row survives, the house on the right (Glen Devon Hotel) set back from the Magistrates' Court and new Police Station block which occupies the site of the other two houses. When the baths closed the building became a skating rink, and after the Great War was converted into a Music Hall and Cinema theatre but it seems that despite various changes in the public entertainment it offered the building was doomed, burning down in a fire a few years after the Second World War.

63. The elegance of Regency Teignmouth catches the eye in this view of Den Crescent around 1900, every bit as pleasing as a classical crescent in Bath. Even the chimney pots have the same careful uniformity in design. The cinema building that we know was then the East Devon & Teignmouth Club with an exclusive membership amongst the gentry and professional middle class. The railings seem to emphasise the limited access. Members could enjoy quiet relaxation in one of the reading rooms, or play billiards, cards or take tea in select company, perhaps on the balcony on a fine day. The balustrade around the balcony has gone; otherwise the exterior of the building has changed very little. Before it was taken over by the Club in 1871 the building had been the town's main Assembly Rooms and lavish balls were held in the 70′ long ballroom. To be left off the invitation list was to be excluded from a prominent social circle, which could be checked in the guest list published in the local newspaper.

64. Before the mid-19th century the Den was a sandy rise on which fishermen had dried their nets for centuries, and this photograph of Powderham Terrace taken in the early 1880's records the ancient right of access to the Den exercised by local fishermen. The dark patches in the foreground are fishing nets laid out to dry on what is now the entrance to the Point car park. This may well be the only photographic record of fishing nets drying on the Den (do readers know of any other?) and yet is left to us by chance as the photographer's main interest was obviously the stylish Powderham Terrace built on the site of fishermen's cottages in the late 1860's. Another piece of luck was that the photograph was rescued just in time from a dustbin, along with the photographs used in plates 3, 21, 35, 52 and 57 and preserved as valuable records of Teignmouth's past by May Bovey.

65. Fishermen are renowned for their yarns of the big ones that got away but the camera never lies. This exceptional catch of salmon in May 1922 is still talked about today. 89 salmon weighing 870 lbs are laid out, and the men went on that day to catch a total of 123. Bob Nathan (Philip's father) is standing at the back, and the others from left to right are Nibby Jarvis, Happy Leyman, Captain Cameron, Bill Shapter, Bill Belton, Char Nathan and Ernie Nathan. On the back of the photograph someone has recorded that the salmon were sold for just £67 1s. per lb, which means that this particular haul of 89 fish brought in £65 5s. to be shared amongst eight men.

Shaldon Motor Ferry, Teignmouth

66. Soon after the turn of the century the boat ride across to Shaldon was much faster with the introduction of motorised ferries, and with the manual burden of the ferryman relieved the boats became larger and the number of passengers on each crossing could be increased. Only five or six people could cross in the smaller rowing ferries. This photograph from around 1910 shows a busy time for the two motorised ferries and also a glimpse of one of the old rowing ferries beached in the centre, all displaying the distinctive black and white design below the gunwales painted to match the 700-ton galleons of Elizabeth I's powerful navy.

67. As this rowing boat lacks the usual black and white design below the gunwales it must be in use as a temporary ferry only, probably carrying important dignitaries and complementing the official ferries on a special occasion in Teignmouth or Shaldon. I am told the ferryman is 'Shrimpy' Mole. The photograph probably dates from 1885-1895 but what the occasion was is unknown and information on the reverse only adds to the intrigue: 'S. Poole, Teignmouth. Photographer to their Royal Highnesses, the Prince & Princess of Wales.' (This was Prince Edward who married Alexandra of Denmark in 1863.) Samuel Poole ran a photographic business in Teignmouth from the late 1850's to the 1890's. He was also a music seller at 2 Somerset Place and the secretary of the Useful Knowledge Society & Mechanics' Institute until the turn of the century. In all probability he was Teignmouth's first professional photographer and also did work for the Devon Photographic Institute and London newspapers.

68. Shaldon Bridge was completely rebuilt in 1930/31 in reinforced concrete and steel, and kept its toll charges for several more years until 1948 when the bridge was taken over by the County Council. Dipping into their pockets or handbags for money was something most foot passengers were reluctant to do after dark and by all accounts there were several ways of nipping over the gate or wall and creeping past the tollkeeper's house without being heard. Built in 1827, the bridge suffered several setbacks. In June 1838 its timbers were discovered to be badly affected by shipworm and the bridge had to be closed for repairs until April 1840, and after a second disaster in 1893 its wooden piers were replaced with iron. Since the bridge was freed from tolls the porch has gone from the tollhouse and the regulations board is now in Teignmouth Museum.

Tea Gardens, "Coombe Cellars", on the River Teign, Teignmouth. Part of Tea Terrace.

69. A summer activity popular with visitors and residents was rowing a boat up the river with Coombe Cellars as the target, and for the man who took the oars what could be more appropriate than a boater hat. Perhaps this river party opted for the skill of local boatsmen instead; they look too elegant to have made it under their own steam. Coombe Cellars offered cockles or cream with tea, taken outside on the tea terrace. Almost 170 years ago Keats wrote of the cream all being spread upon barley bread. A game of skittles was also part of the outing. 'Everybody who goes to the cellars plays skittles,' wrote Beatrix Cresswell in 1901. The licensee then was W. James, the business changing hands before the Great War to Henry George Stigings who ran it for many years after.

70. The leisured class enjoying their cockles at Coombe Cellars were privileged indeed. A holiday away from home was quite unknown to the majority, unless they were servants accompanying a rich family. The other side of the coin was poverty and a hard life, readily obvious in the weather-beaten face of this old cockle woman photographed using her cockle rake at nearby Starcross before the Great War. Although she looks elderly to us she may be in no more than her fifties. She calls to mind the description of Teignmouth fisherwomen penned by Fanny Burney in 1773: *Their dress is barbarous. They have stays half-laced and something by way of handkerchiefs about their necks, they wear one coloured flannel or stuff petticoat; no shoes or stockings, not withstanding the hard pebbles and stones all along the beach; their coat is pinned up in the shape of a pair of trousers leaving them wholly naked to the knee.*

71. The picnic party at the top of Breakneck Hill around 1905 saw many more open fields than exist now. The nearest construction work to them is the Hazeldown reservoir halfway down on the right. Maudlin Drive and the Ashleigh housing estate now occupy most of these meadows, and Coombe Valley on the other side of Exeter Road is also built up. Note the narrower, hedged Exeter Road of those days. Travellers arriving this way on a cold, dark night had no bright pools of electric light and road signs in luminous paint to guide them, just the distant blue glow of gas lamps in the town below, always assuming they could see them through the clouds of chimney smoke. Newspapers of the time carried frequent reports of chimneys on fire and invariably the householder was prosecuted.

72. At the turn of the century Teignmothians knew the Exeter Road as 'pretty, shady, with some handsome residences on either side, and a fine prospect of sea and country as it ascends to the Cemetery' (Beatrix Cresswell). There were virtually no buildings after Yannon Terrace, and Coombe Valley consisted of 'thatched farms and meadowy orchards sheltered in the hollow'. This picture shows the area below Hazeldown reservoir (right foreground) in more detail than plate 71, with Trinity School on the left and the cemetery on the right. Yannon Terrace is several fields below the cemetery. Like the gasworks the cemetery was built on the outskirts of the town, and had anyone envisaged how the town would develop in our time the several acres of cemetery land would no doubt have been reserved for housing. It started off as a tiny 2-acre site with two mortuary chapels in 1856 costing £2,500.

73. Taken from St. Michael's tower before the Great War, this photograph shows an unusual view of the Dawlish Road with the United Reformed Church and Roman Catholic church on the left. The large house amongst the trees on the right is where the coach park now lies, and the fields in the distance have become the housing estate north of New Road. Just to the left of the United Reformed Church in the foreground there is a tiny glimpse of the old Teignmouth Hospital on the site now occupied by the new Alberta Court dwellings and, tinier still, two washerwomen are struggling up the middle of the road with a large wicker basket – and not a vehicle in sight.

74. By the late 1920's it was no longer necessary to climb Breakneck Hill or St. Michael's tower for aerial views of the town. Ken Cook, outside his parents' greengrocers' shop at 38 Northumberland Place between 1926 and 1929, saw the early days of flying from Haldon aerodrome. He remembers being fascinated by the sight of an Avro-Avion aircraft with its folding wings being manoeuvred into Gilpin's Garage (now Central Garage). There was a loudspeaker above the garage which used to broadcast news of national interest for those without their own wireless set, and people would gather to hear election results and the results of the Derby. Eventually the BBC stopped direct broadcasting of this kind, having themselves put so much effort into gathering the news.

75. This 1930 family snapshot provides a record of the Teignmouth Motor Car Company whose hoardings and booking office were by the Post Office (a shop has since been built right of the doorway and on its left there is an amusement arcade). On offer are trips to Haytor, Becky Falls, Princetown, Dartmeet and Plymouth, and the company also ran the town service and a bus service to Haldon. In 1930 the proprietors were G. Rossiter and H. Fraser, and previously the company had been owned by William Burden, the ironmonger and RNLI secretary. However, they were not without competitors and in 1936 they were taken over by their larger rivals, the Devon General bus company. The two ladies in the foreground are from Exeter enjoying a day trip to the town.

DEN PROMENADE AND PIER, TEIGNMOUTH

76. In the preceding pages we have followed the promenaders in their 'Sunday best' to the Teignmouth of horse-drawn transport, gas lighting and the discreet bathing machine, and this ornately bordered photograph taken around 1900 serves as a porthole on a time very different from our own. Yet it dates from our own century. It is likely, but nonetheless jolting, that the children skipping towards us lived to know of manned space flight, digital watches and credit card shopping. They could point out that the Victorian and Edwardian age was also the age of many other things: high infant mortality, women without a political voice and desperate poverty for many. However, the Teignmothians who talk of those times recall above all the fun that people made for themselves and a town with a proud past.